SERVICE HEROES IN HOSPITALITY: A GUEST SERVICE TRAINING PROGRAM

Participant Book

Name _____

Ben A. Sharpton

© 1999, BEN A. SHARPTON

Copyright © 1999, Ben Sharpton

All rights reserved. Any reproduction of this material in any media without written permission of the publisher is a violation of United States copyright law.

Published by: HRD Press, Inc.
22 Amherst Road
Amherst, MA 01002
800-822-2801 (U.S. and Canada)
413-253-3488
413-253-3490 (fax)
http://www.hrdpress.com

ISBN # 0-87425-468-X

Design services by CompuDesign
Cover design by Eileen Klockars
Editorial services by Suzanne Bay

TABLE OF CONTENTS

MODULE 1: WELCOME TO YOUR FUTURE!
- Overview 7
- Objectives of Module 1................................ 8
- Service Profile... 9
- Scoring the Service Profile........................ 14
- Service Profile Explanation 15
- Expectations 16
- What Did You Expect?............................... 17

MODULE 2: SEVEN SERVICE ADVANTAGES
- Overview 21
- Objectives of Module 2.............................. 22
- Seven Service Advantages 23
- Case Study: A Night to Remember 24
- Case Study: One of those Days.................. 26
- Examples of the Seven Service Advantages 28

MODULE 3: SERVICE SITUATIONS
- Overview 31
- Objectives of Module 3.............................. 32
- Making Sense 33
- Personal Guidelines.................................. 34
- Service Situations 35

MODULE 4: BOUNCING BACK
- Overview 41
- Objectives of Module 4.............................. 42
- GREAT Guest Service................................ 43
- Tough Situations—Restaurant Industry 44
- Tough Situations—Hotel Industry.............. 46

MODULE 5: BECOMING STRATEGIC PARTNERS
- Overview 51
- Objectives of Module 5.............................. 52
- Fill in the Blanks...................................... 53
- Service Heoes We Have Known and Loved ... 54
- Self Assessment....................................... 55
- Service Heroes Evaluation Form................ 56

RESOURCES FOR SERVICE HEROES
- Books 57
- Internet Sites... 57

Dedication

Back in the 1950's, 60's, 70's and 80's my father was a successful automobile dealer. He succeeded in difficult years for American automobile dealers because his business was based on service. "Ride Satisfied" and "Recommended by your friends" were his mottos. This program is dedicated to Dad, with sincere thanks for introducing me to service.

My appreciation also goes to Dr. Rick Bommelje, my professor at Rollins College who constantly encouraged me to seek the best way and the best way to explain what I'd discovered.

My gratitude also goes to my wife, Kay, who has always provided me with time and emotional support to put my thoughts and dreams on paper. Her service has allowed me to teach others to serve.

MODULE 1:

WELCOME TO YOUR FUTURE!

OVERVIEW

You've probably noticed a change in yourself recently. You've become more demanding. You expect more from the places you shop, the restaurants you choose to dine in, and the places you visit with your family and friends. You insist that those who work in such establishments treat you with respect, and you want to be pleasantly surprised by excellent service.

Well, you're not alone. The same changes are taking place all around the world. Customers now believe that price and quality are no longer enough to win them over. They want to be valued as important customers, and if *you* can't provide the service they believe they deserve, there's a competitor of yours right down the street who can.

The hospitality industry is demanding and competitive. People who use your services have high expectations and, like you, they insist on getting what they pay for.

You can surprise your guests with exceptional service. In fact, you can exceed their expectations! At the beginning of each and every day, you *know* you can make a difference in the pleasure and comfort of your guests—that's one reason why this is such a unique business. When you are able to turn an average experience into one that is better than they expected, you become a kind of hero to your guests.

Service Heroes is designed to help you and the other participants in this program discover ways to make a real impact on guests' experiences. You'll identify your own reasons for providing service, and discover some special tips to make your service more effective than it is now. You'll learn how to handle guests who are upset. And you'll have a bit of fun with a great group of people.

Welcome, Service Hero.

"Do you want know how bad customer service is these days? If I wasn't doing this show, *I* would be a customer service representative."

Dennis Miller
"Rant" on HBO
May 29, 1998

"Trying to find a customer service department in 1998 America is like trying to find a clock in a casino. Between the catatonic indifference and the Nurse Ratchett-like attitude, you have a better chance of winning the Publisher's Clearinghouse Sweepstakes, finding the Holy Grail in your garage and finding the lost City of Atlantis in your septic tank all in one day, than you do of finding one . . . human being out there who can help you with anything!"

Dennis Miller
"Rant" on HBO
May 29, 1998

OBJECTIVES OF MODULE 1

By the end of this module, participants will:

- Be able to state why they strive to provide excellent service.

- Begin thinking of new ways to provide service.

- Understand the importance of service today.

SERVICE PROFILE

Take a quick look at each of the following service scenarios. Each is followed by a single question with several possible answers. Select the answer that most realistically fits the situation by placing a check mark in the appropriate box. There are no right or wrong answers, so be honest in your selection.

Situation #1: George has been a bellman at your hotel for three years. He always greets each person who stays at the hotel with a big smile and a hearty, "Greetings!" He chats with some of them while they wait for their cars. He's always willing to give directions.

What would motivate you to treat guests the way George treats guests?

- ❒ The possibility of receiving a better tip.
- △ The understanding that management wants me to act that way.
- ○ I enjoy making people happy.

Situation #2: Sharlene is a new waitress in the restaurant. She really seems to hustle to get the food from the kitchen to the table. Twice today she almost ran over another waiter by accident. She smiles a lot at the guests, and chats briefly with them when not busy.

What would motivate you to model your service after Sharlene's?

- ○ I am happy when those around me are happy.
- ❒ I need a good job.
- △ Some sort of team incentive or contest.

SERVICE PROFILE

Situation #3: Your manager just called the staff together and read a letter from a guest who visited recently. The guest pointed out how Margarita went out of her way to make sure that the guest had a great experience. "If I looked in the dictionary under 'service,' I think I'd find Margarita's name," the guest said in the letter.

If you were to receive such recognition, what would have motivated you?

- ❐ The hope that a guest would write a complimentary letter like the one the manager just read.
- △ Margarita's not alone. She treats guests well, just like the rest of the team.
- ○ I just like to help people in this way.

Situation #4: The lobby is empty. The first rush of the day is over, and most of the employees are catching their breath, getting ready for the second onslaught. Tom, however, is walking around the lobby, picking up scraps of paper and tidying up.

What would cause you to work to keep the place clean, like Tom?

- △ Tom's just doing his job. Next time, someone else will be responsible for picking up trash.
- ❐ I want to make a good impression on the manager who is probably watching me.
- ○ I would clean up because of the pride I have in my job and my company.

SERVICE PROFILE

Situation #5: Everyone is exhausted and ready for a break when a group of three families (with five toddlers) enters the restaurant for dinner. This group is definitely a high-maintenance group. Jeff tells the hostess that he will take care of the large group.

What would have motivated you to volunteer to take care of the group?

- ○ Everyone deserves good service and I can take the best care of these families.
- ❏ I know families tend to be big tippers. Besides, I like kids.
- △ It's my turn to take a large group.

Situation #6: Rose has worked in the hotel for several years. She doesn't complain. She doesn't argue. She quietly and efficiently cleans rooms every day. Sometimes she goes out of her way to take care of guests. As you're getting ready to go home, you notice Rose running up to a room with an armload of towels. "They were going to the beach today. They'll need these when they return," you hear her say.

What would cause you to show such personal concern for guests?

- ❏ I am hoping that this family will notice and leave a nice tip.
- ○ I just enjoy making other people happy.
- △ All housekeepers are taught to provide extra towels when necessary.

SERVICE PROFILE

Situation #7: The convention starts tomorrow and everyone has worked late to set up. After moving hundreds of tables and about a thousand chairs, you collapse in one of the last chairs you moved. Looking up, you see Larry climbing a ladder to straighten the pipe and drape beside one of the displays.

What would cause you to climb the ladder as Larry did?

- ○ I feel that everything I am involved with should be as good as possible.
- ▫ I like the company that owns the display and can get a sample of their product in return for my extra effort.
- △ I know that management expects everyone to go above and beyond the call of duty.

Situation #8: Sarah opened a box of children's breakfast cereal and gave it to a family with a young infant while their meal was being prepared. It helped quiet the noisy child.

What would help you decide to act in a similar way?

- △ My manager suggested that giving away a small box of cereal might be a good way to get parents to spend more.
- ▫ Silence! I think it might keep the infant quiet.
- ○ Giving away cereal is one way I can exceed guest expectations.

SERVICE PROFILE

Situation #9: Kip drew a map so some guests could take a short cut to get to a nearby theater in time for the show. He could have given them the regular directions without a map, but they might have arrived late.

What would cause you to go to such lengths to ensure that the guests get to a movie before it starts?

- ❒ I'm hoping to impress one of the girls/boys in the party.
- ◯ I understand that the guests really want to see this show, and I want to help them get what they want.
- △ An incentive contest might make me try to win points for my team.

Situation #10: Mary brings delicious homemade brownies for the staff every Friday.

Why would you be extra nice to "internal guests"—your fellow employees?

- ◯ If I knew how to bake, I would enjoy sharing my talents with others.
- ❒ So the people I work with will like me. Besides, I get hungry every now and then and would like a snack.
- △ Everyone on the team treats one another like this all the time.

SCORING THE SERVICE PROFILE

Take a close look at your answers and add up the number of check marks in each symbol. Write the number of *check marks* in the square boxes in the large *bronze* box below. Write the number of check marks in the triangles in the large *silver* triangle and the number of check marks in the circles in the large *gold* circle.

Bronze   Silver   Gold

Service Profile Explanation

People provide service for a number of different reasons. Some do so in hopes of receiving something in return. Others do so because management expects them to. Others enjoy making people happy. What is important is to understand why *you* do it.

All of the responses in the "bronze" boxes indicate that someone expects to receive a personal benefit when providing the service. If receiving a reward or avoiding punishment is important to you, you probably checked this box. Bronze Service Providers usually ask the question, "What's in it for me?"

The responses in the "silver" triangles indicate that the group's rules or the team's practices suggested the service action. If your group tends to be service-oriented, or if your management insists that employees provide unusual service, you are likely to provide good service. Silver Service Providers ask, "What does the team or the company want me to do?"

The responses next to the "gold" circles are ones in which service is provided because people believe in the principle of service: they provide service because service is very important to them. If you checked "gold" boxes, service is one way that you can make others happy. Gold Service Providers look for ways to exceed guest expectations because they take pride in their work and enjoy taking care of guests.

One study indicated that waitresses who wrote "Thank You" at the bottom of their customers' tickets received an average of 2% more in tips than those who did not. Another study showed that waitresses who drew happy faces on their tickets received as much as 5% more in tips than those who did not. However, men who drew happy faces received less in tips than men who did not.

EXPECTATIONS

Team A

Things don't always happen the way we would like them to. Sometimes we fail to meet our guests' expectations. On the following lines, list as many occurrences as you can in your work area that would be *below* a guest's expectations:

_____ _____

_____ _____

_____ _____

_____ _____

_____ _____

_____ _____

_____ _____

Team B

Sometimes we're able to surprise guests with service that they never expected. On the following lines, list as many occurrences as you can that are likely to be *above* a guest's expectations:

_____ _____

_____ _____

_____ _____

_____ _____

_____ _____

_____ _____

_____ _____

WHAT DID YOU EXPECT?

It all comes down to a matter of expectations. Guests purchase a service from our company. In return, they have certain expectations—they want to know that they got what they paid for. If we fail to meet those expectations, guests will be disappointed. If we exceed their expectations, guests will think that they made a wise decision.

Think about the case of Great Expectations. Every time Mr. Dickens gets less than he expected, deduct Expectation Points from your total score. When Mr. Dickens gets more than he expected, add Expectation Points to your total score. Total all the points to arrive at your TOTAL E-Point score.

Great Expectations

Enter Lobby, Greeted by employee	_____ E-Points
Short lines, brief waits	_____ E-Points
Courteous desk clerk	_____ E-Points
No surprises on the price	_____ E-Points
Easy access to room	_____ E-Points
Clean and tidy room	_____ E-Points
Lights turned on for reading	_____ E-Points
TOTAL:	_____ **E-Points**

How might a guest respond when. . . (Write in your thoughts).

We disappoint them.   We exceed their expectations.

_____   _____

_____   _____

_____   _____

> "The secret of joy in work is contained in one word—excellence. To know how to do something well is to enjoy it."
>
> —Pearl Buck,
> American Novelist

MODULE 2:

SEVEN SERVICE ADVANTAGES

OVERVIEW

Coaches look for athletes who have certain size, speed or agility advantages over their opponents, and who work to make the most of these advantages. Marketing professionals work to demonstrate the advantages their product has that the competition lacks. Political candidates try to demonstrate the advantages they have over their opponents when running for office.

Service Advantages are the things we do and the perspectives we have that set us apart from the other businesses competing for guests. They give us the edge to out-service our competition.

The Seven Service Advantages are skills we can each develop. They are not difficult. They are not even unusual. The first step in exceeding guest expectations is to begin to exercise the Seven Service Advantages.

> "What we're trying to do is nothing more than what we try to teach our children. Good manners, be polite, be pleasant, treat anybody the way you'd like to be treated yourself, is really what we must put across."
>
> —Isadore Sharp, former CEO of Four Seasons Hotels

OBJECTIVES OF MODULE 2:

By the end of this module, participants will:

- Understand the seven strategies that Service Heroes use to their advantage when providing service.

- Know how to meet each of the Service Advantages.

Seven Service Advantages

Seven things set Service Heroes apart from the rest of the people who provide service. These are advantages they have that other people don't use. Service Heroes make the most of the following "Service Advantages" as they interact with guests. Use the space to record your own thoughts about the following service advantages:

1. The Guest Perspective:
   _____
   _____
   _____

2. The Element of Surprise!
   _____
   _____
   _____

3. The Ability to Anticipate Guest Needs:
   _____
   _____
   _____

4. A Personal Touch:
   _____
   _____
   _____

5. Courtesy:
   _____
   _____
   _____

6. Listening:
   _____
   _____
   _____

7. Fun!
   _____
   _____
   _____

"Advantage: The first point scored after deuce, or the resulting state of the score in tennis."

—The American College Dictionary

CASE STUDY: A NIGHT TO REMEMBER...
(Restaurant Industry)

Guest Perspective

"Smith, family of four." The call came over the restaurant's PA system. A weary-looking family dragged up to the hostess stand.

Courtesy

"Good evening!" the hostess exclaimed. "My, you look hungry. You came to the right place. Follow me."

Element of Surprise

As they walked to their booth, the hostess asked about their day.

"What a day," Bill started. "We got on a plane before dawn, flew into town, lost our luggage, had a flat tire on the rental car, got sunburned on the beach, and then got lost trying to find the hotel."

"I'm so sorry," the hostess said. "I imagine you're thirsty, so I'll see that you get some water while you look at the menu."

Within a few moments, the waitress appeared with three tall glasses of ice water and a plastic cup of water covered by a lid. She placed the cup in front of the Smith's three-year-old.

Listening

Sarah Smith was writing a post card when the waitress approached. Noting that Sarah was a "lefty," the waitress placed her glass near the left side of her plate.

"I'm so hungry, I could eat a cow," Bill said.

Ability to Anticipate Guest Needs

"Then you'll probably want the Roast Beef Special," the waitress offered. "On the other hand, if you're still feeling warm from the beach, you might consider the seafood salad."

When she brought their dinners, the waitress placed some extra paper napkins on the table. Knowing how messy some children can be, she thought they might come in handy. As she placed dinner on the table she asked how everyone enjoyed the beach. She listened intently as eight-year-old Kathy talked about hunting for shells. After she finished, the hostess suggested to Bill that they might try another beach, just a

Case Study: A Night to Remember...
(Restaurant Industry)

couple of miles down the road. "The locals go there because the shelling is supposed to be better," she said.

Knowing that people with sunburn tend to chill easily, the hostess brought a sweater to the table and offered it to Kathy and Sarah. Kathy gratefully accepted it and wrapped it around Sarah's shoulders.

As the waitress brought the check, Kathy was telling an intense story about a program on scuba diving that she'd seen on television. The waitress waited until Kathy stopped talking to ask if the family wanted anything else. Sarah mentioned that little Bill still seemed thirsty, so the waitress suggested that she refill his cup and let Bill take it. In a few moments, she returned with the fresh cup of ice water.

Fun!

As they were walking into the lobby, the hostess approached them again. "You mentioned that you and your family had gotten sunburned at the beach," she started. "If you want to pick up some sunburn ointment, there's a 24-hour pharmacy just about three blocks down the street on the right."

Personal Touch

Walking through the parking lot, Bill placed his arm around Sarah's waist and said, "You know, I'd like to come back here again."

Case Study: One of Those Days...
(Hotel Industry)

Guest Perspective

The Ellis family entered the hotel lobby like a hurricane. Todd, Kevin, and Jeremy ran over to the "Local Attractions" brochure rack and began to snatch up as many colorful advertisements as they could carry.

Courtesy

June hurried to catch her sons. "Just one of each brochure, kids," she said.

Tom stepped up to the counter, "We need a room . . . or a suite . . . make that an entire wing."

"Do you have a reservation?" Sarah, the desk clerk, asked as her fingers quickly tapped on the computer keyboard.

Element of Surprise

"No," Tom answered. "I'm afraid not. We were at another hotel up the street and had to, er, decided to leave."

Todd folded one of the brochures into an airplane and launched it across the lobby. Kevin and Jeremy quickly imitated their brother.

Listening

"We have a suite on the third floor," the desk clerk said.

"Is that a smoking room? I really need a cigarette."

"Tom," June interrupted. "Remember Jeremy's allergies."

"Well, better make it a non-smoking room," Tom said.

"Still got a headache, Dad?" Kevin asked. Tom nodded, in obvious anguish.

Ability to Anticipate Guest Needs

"I can place you near the swimming pool," Sarah suggested. "The boys would probably like that."

As Sarah handed over the room keys she mentioned, "All of our rooms have in-room movies. Would you like us to block out 'R-rated' movies?"

"You bet," June said.

Case Study: One of Those Days...

(Hotel Industry)

Tom frowned.

"There are two TV's in the suite. Why don't you call me when you decide which room will be yours and I won't block those channels on your set."

"Do you have room service?" Tom asked. "I'm starving."

"Our room service is quite good," Sarah responded, handing him a copy of the menu. "Just call the number at the bottom."

Fun!

The noise level in the lobby was beginning to rise to near-deafening levels. "Do you guys like pizza?" Sarah asked the three boisterous boys.

"Yeah!" they answered in unison.

Personal Touch

"We've got the best pizza in the city. Just talk with your parents."

"Thanks," Tom said, as he began to herd his family toward the door.

"If there is anything we can do, just let us know," Karen answered. "Oh, Mr. Ellis. Here's a package of complimentary aspirin. If you prefer something else, our gift store is open until 9:00."

Tom gratefully accepted the aspirin and then turned to his wife as they walked out the door. "You know, we should have come to this hotel first."

Examples of the Seven Service Advantages

Brainstorm together with the other members of your group and list as many ways you can think of to meet one of the Service Advantages.

The Guest Perspective

_____

_____

_____

_____

The Element of Surprise!

_____

_____

_____

_____

The Ability to Anticipate Guest Needs

_____

_____

_____

_____

A Personal Touch

_____

_____

_____

_____

Courtesy

_____

_____

_____

_____

Listening

_____

_____

_____

_____

Fun!

_____

_____

_____

_____

_____

MODULE 3:

SERVICE SITUATIONS

OVERVIEW

Service Heroes look for opportunities to do more than a guest expects, often with no flash or fanfare. The skill of exceeding expectations requires a combination of common sense and sensitivity.

Objectives of Module 3

By the end of this module, participants will:

- Know how to provide outstanding service in specific on-the-job situations.

- Be able to demonstrate exemplary service behavior.

MAKING SENSE

On the lines below, list those things that might exceed guest expectations in your work area. Use the topic headings (the five senses) to trigger some of your thoughts.

Name of Your Work Area: _____

Sight: _____
_____
_____

Hearing: _____
_____
_____

Taste: _____
_____
_____

Smell: _____
_____
_____

Touch: _____
_____
_____

Does Service Make A Difference?

One industry study revealed that when grocery store attendants provided more courteous behavior to customers—smiles, eye contact, leaning forward to listen, etc. their customers indicated that they would return to the store and that they would even pass other stores to shop at this one.

PERSONAL GUIDELINES

Work with your partner to create your own set of personal guidelines, those rules that you will use to remind yourself of ways that you can exceed guest expectations. Use the following headings to organize your thoughts:

When greeting a guest . . .

_____

_____

_____

When a guest enters the room . . .

_____

_____

_____

When a guest asks a question . . .

_____

_____

_____

When a guest is disappointed . . .

_____

_____

_____

When a guest leaves . . .

_____

_____

_____

SERVICE SITUATIONS

Read through the Role Play Situation that your group has been assigned and create two role plays based on that scenario. One role play should demonstrate either average or poor guest service (you choose). The second role play should demonstrate outstanding guest service in the same situation.

Role Play #1: The Confused Family

It's 10:45 p.m. and a family stumbles into the lobby, tired and dreary. The father approaches the reservation desk and announces that his name is Bill Fuddle and that he has a reservation. The desk clerk checks the computer but does not find the reservation. Mr. Fuddle digs through his pockets for the reservation number, while his wife begins to berate him about not making the reservation. Their son (or daughter) begins to complain.

Finally, Mr. Fuddle finds the reservation number and gives it to the desk clerk. Again the clerk checks the computer and finds that a B. Fuddle has a reservation in a sister hotel on the opposite side of town (about one hour away). Mrs. Fuddle continues to nag her husband, and their son (or daughter) begins to cry.

Just then, the Regional Manager calls on the phone and insists on having the current ADR (Average Daily Rate report).

What can the desk clerk do to help the B. Fuddle family?

Players: Desk Clerk
Bill Fuddle
Mary Fuddle
Billy Fuddle (or Mary Lou Fuddle)

"Businesses planned for service are apt to succeed; businesses planned for profit are apt to fail."

—Nicholas M. Butler

SERVICE SITUATIONS

Role Play #2: QUIET!

Franklyn Noyce is staying in room 855 in the hotel. He has a major sales presentation to make at 6:30 a.m. tomorrow morning. He's tired from the four-hour flight and wants to get some rest.

The Springdale High School Marching Band is also staying in the hotel. They're in rooms 840 through 853. The band just won the state marching band contest, and the kids want to celebrate.

Mr. Noyce approaches the front desk at 2:30 a.m. He's called the front desk three times, but cannot get anyone to quiet down the noisy guests on the 8th floor. He asks the desk clerk for help.

The desk clerk began the late shift at 2:00 a.m., and did not know of Mr. Noyce's problem until now.

What can the desk clerk do to help Mr. Noyce?

    Players: Desk Clerk

                      Bellman (or Security Officer, or Night Auditor)

                      Franklyn Noyce (salesman)

                      Tommy Parker (Springdale High School Marching Band trombone player)

                      George Malone (Springdale High School Marching Band base drummer)

Service Situations

Role Play #3: Cold Pizza

Robert and Barbara Barberra call the waiter (or waitress) to their table. They are upset because the pizza they ordered is cold.

Robert says he wants to see the manager. He also says the pizza sauce tastes sour.

Barbara doesn't want to complain. She says she would be happy if the waiter just brought a fresh, hot pizza.

The waiter looks at the table and notices that the Barberras have eaten six of the eight slices.

What can the waiter (and the manager, if necessary) do to help the Barberras?

    Players: Waiter (or Waitress)

                    Anthony Barberra

                    Rosa Barberra

NOTE: If you work in a hotel, you can do the same role play using a room service scenario.

Role Play #4: Greasy Palms at the Greasy Spoon

David and Susanne are on their first date and they've chosen the elegant "Seafood Cellar" for dinner. The hostess asks if they have a reservation and David realizes that he forgot to make one. The restaurant is packed.

Susanne is starving (she's dieted for a week in preparation for this date) and is becoming faint. Hoping to impress her, David attempts to slip the hostess ten dollars in exchange for a seat in the restaurant.

What should the hostess do to help David and Susanne?

    Players: Hostess

                    Susanne

                    David

Service Situations

Role Play #5: Nothing Personal

Rob enters a fast food restaurant and orders a hamburger, fries and a soft drink. The lady behind the counter takes his order and calls him "Honey." Moments later, she gives him change and calls him "Sugar."

Obviously, these pet names irritate Rob. However, Rob believes she is just trying, in her own way, to be pleasant.

She presents Rob's order and says, "Y'all take care, sweetie."

Rob sits down at the farthest table from the cash register and examines his order. The fries are missing.

He approaches the counter and complains that he has been short-changed, and he asks to see the Manager.

What can the Manager do to help Rob?

    Players: Counter Clerk

                          Rob

                          Manager

MODULE 4:

BOUNCING BACK

OVERVIEW

When things go wrong, what you do and what you say almost always speaks louder than what happened. Most guests can be very forgiving, if proper action is taken quickly. Service recovery is somewhat like a mended broken bone. When you surprise guests with a thoughtful and speedy recovery, you win back their support. In fact, their support is often stronger than it was before.

OBJECTIVES OF MODULE 4

Why companies lose customers:

They die 1%

They move........... 3%

They have been persuaded by friends ... 5%

They were lured away by competition ... 9%

They were dissatisfied with the product 14%

They were turned away by an attitude of indifference on the part of a company employee 68%

—The American Society for Quality Control

By the end of this module, participants will:

- Understand why it is important to recover from service failures quickly.

- View complaining guests as their strongest allies.

- Be able to list five steps to take when dealing with an upset guest.

GREAT Guest Service

Good guest service is necessary to meet guest expectations. But GREAT guest service helps you exceed expectations and turn a guest's day around after a service disappointment. The elements of GREAT guest service are:

- **G**reet the guest/**G**ather information

- **R**eassure the guest that you'll take care of the situation

- **E**xamine the alternatives

- **A**ct to resolve the issues

- **T**hank the guest

"The price of greatness is responsibility."

—Winston Churchill

Tough Situations—Restaurant Industry

Take a look at each of the following "Tough Situations" for restaurant personnel. Choose one that is most similar to the work you and your teammates do and write in the words you would say for each stage of GREAT guest service. One of the members of your team should be ready to share the responses with the rest of the group.

Situation	GREAT Service Steps (what you'd say/do)
Tough Situation for Waiters/Waitresses A couple and their four-year-old child are upset because their order seems to be taking too long. They want to get to the mall before it closes, but now they don't think they will make it. They asked for water ten minutes ago, but no one brought them any. They say they've never seen such poor service and would like to talk with the manager, but they doubt that he or she cares enough to listen.	G _____ R _____ E _____ A _____ T _____

TOUGH SITUATIONS— RESTAURANT INDUSTRY

Situation	GREAT Service Steps (what you'd say/do)
Tough Situation for Hosts and Hostesses Three non-smoking guests have been waiting for over 30 minutes for a table. When they arrived, they were told the wait would be 20 minutes, but some of the other guests stayed longer than expected and a busser went home sick, so things aren't clean yet. They aren't interested in sitting in the bar (too smoky), and feel that they were lied to when they came in.	G _____ R _____ E _____ A _____ T _____
Tough Situation for Table Bussers A family of three has been dining in one of your booths for over 45 minutes. Their three-year-old has scattered french fries, bread crumbs and something else (you're not really sure what) all over the floor beneath the high chair. Twice, the child spilled his water. Now, the father is complaining that their table is sticky, and the mother is complaining that the booth feels "dirty."	G _____ R _____ E _____ A _____ T _____

TOUGH SITUATIONS— HOTEL INDUSTRY

Take a look at each of the following "Tough Situations" for hotel personnel. Choose one that is most similar to the work you and your teammates do and write in the words you would say for each stage of GREAT guest service. One of the members of your team should be ready to share the responses with the rest of the group.

Situation	GREAT Service Steps (what you'd say/do)
Hotel Desk Clerks The elderly gentleman standing in front of you swears that he was quoted a rate half as much as your lowest current rate. He also says he was to stay in a non-smoking room on the first floor, as far away from the pool as possible. You check his room listing and find that he is in a smoking wing on the fourth floor overlooking the pool.	G _____ R _____ E _____ A _____ T _____

Tough Situations—Hotel Industry

Situation	GREAT Service Steps (what you'd say/do)
Housekeepers The hotel is packed. You've just knocked on the door of the last room on your floor and you find that guests who were supposed to check out today are still here. You remind them of the check-out time and they "remind" you that they told you yesterday that they'd be staying another day. You don't remember that conversation. The new guests are waiting in the lobby for this room.	G _____ R _____ E _____ A _____ T _____
Bellmen and Parking Attendants A guest has asked for directions to a nearby restaurant. You've spelled it out for him three times already, and he still doesn't understand. He's beginning to get frustrated and begins to tell you that you're just "playin' him for a fool." He says he knows the general manager and that he'll have your job for treating him this way. He's starting to make a lot of noise and create a scene.	G _____ R _____ E _____ A _____ T _____

MODULE 5:

BECOMING STRATEGIC PARTNERS

OVERVIEW

In the future, the organizations that will survive and thrive will be those that can foster loyalty among employees. Service Heroes envision themselves as integral parts of their organization. They talk about *their* restaurant, *their* hotel, *their* floor, and *their* rooms. They take responsibility for whatever happens while they are on watch. They see themselves as strategic partners in their organizations.

Objectives of Module 5

By the end of this module, participants will:

- View themselves as strategic players in their organization's success.

- Feel confident about their own individual ability to do their job and provide outstanding service.

- Commit to seeking opportunities to provide exemplary service to guests.

FILL IN THE BLANKS

When you provide great service to guests, what two or three things do you do very well?

1. _____

2. _____

3. _____

Now write down the two or three job responsibilities that you do the best.

1. _____

2. _____

3. _____

Imagine for a second that you are the head of this company (CEO, President, "Big Cheese," etc.) What would you do?

_____

_____

_____

Okay, Mr. or Ms. CEO. Now, imagine that you decide not to tell anybody that you're the "Big Cheese." You've decided to continue to do the same job you are now doing for another month. What would you do differently on the job?

_____

_____

_____

"Think like a guest. Act like the owner."

Blaine Sweatt
Creator of Olive Garden
and Bahama Breeze
restaurants

Service Heroes We Have Known and Loved

Think of someone you know who really is a Service Hero. Fill in the following information about him or her:

Name: _____

Occupation: _____

Length of time on job: _____

What does this person do that makes them a Service Hero?

_____
_____
_____
_____

Self Assessment

Think over the concepts you have learned in this course. What specific practices do you need to adopt in order to be a better service provider? Write them down and place a check mark next to what you should put into practice within the next month.

The Service Hero Suggestion Box

- ☐ _____
- ☐ _____
- ☐ _____
- ☐ _____
- ☐ _____
- ☐ _____

SERVICE HEROES EVALUATION FORM

Thank you for participating in our Service Heroes in Hospitality class. As you know, feedback from guests is vital if we are to provide the best service. Feedback from *you* is vital if we are to provide the best class on guest service. Please take a few moments to complete the following evaluation by placing a check mark in the appropriate box.

The ideas taught in this class will help me provide better services to our guests.

☐ Yes ☐ ☐ ☐ ☐ No

I have a better understanding of why I should provide outstanding service to our guests.

☐ Yes ☐ ☐ ☐ ☐ No

I feel better equipped to handle tough guest situations.

☐ Yes ☐ ☐ ☐ ☐ No

The Trainer kept everyone involved during the class.

☐ Yes ☐ ☐ ☐ ☐ No

The Trainer used good presentation skills.

☐ Yes ☐ ☐ ☐ ☐ No

I would recommend this class to others in our company.

☐ Yes ☐ ☐ ☐ ☐ No

Name: _____ (Optional)

Resources for Service Heroes

Books:

The Customer Comes Second, by Hal Rosenbluth and Diane McFerrin Peters. New York: Quill William Morrow, 1992.

Service America! by Karl Albrecht and Ron Zemke. New York: Dow Jones-Irwin, 1990.

Knock Your Socks Off Service, by Ron Zemke.

Managing Knock Your Socks Off Service, by Chip Bell and Ron Zemke. New York: Performance Research Associates, Inc. AMACOM American Management Association, 1993.

Sustaining Knock Your Socks Off Service, by Thomas Connellan and Ron Zemke. New York: Performance Research Associates, Inc., AMACOM American Management Association, 1992.

Positively Outrageous Service, by T. Scott Gross. New York: Mastermedia Limited, 1992.

Send This Jerk The Bedbug Letter, by John Bear, Ph. D. Berkeley, CA: Ten Speed Press, 1996.

Internet Sites:

Customer Edge daily email newsletter: http://www.customeredge.com/subscribe.htm

Courtesy Please website: http://www.4dcomm.com:80/~slstcp

First Rate Customer Service website (newsletter): http://www.geocities.com

Customer Service Review: http://WWW.CSR.CO.ZA

The Right Answer webpage: http://www.therightanswer.com

Customer Service Review webpage: http://www.csr.co.za/

TARP Customer Care Solutions webpage: http://www.tarp.com/

About the Author

Ben Sharpton has spent the last twelve years designing corporate training and development programs. As Manager of Training Design for Universal Studios Escape in Orlando, Florida, a leader in the theme park industry, he is responsible for the design and presentation of management development/customer service workshops and seminars for Universal's 6,000 Florida employees. A $2 billion dollar expansion will enlarge the workforce at Universal Studios-Escape to 15,000 employees in the next two years' time.

Before joining Universal, Mr. Sharpton spent seven years at Tupperware Worldwide Headquarters, where he designed sales, customer service, technical, and operational programs for the company's nationwide consultants and distributors.

A prolific freelance writer, Mr. Sharpton has received six Florida Freelance Writers Contest awards. His work has appeared in more than 40 books and magazines, including *Entrepreneur*, *Secrets of Success*, and *Apple Direct*, with more than 130 published credits.

Mr. Sharpton holds a Master of Arts degree in Human Resources Management from Rollins College, a Master of Arts degree from Wheaton College, and a Bachelor of Arts degree from Asbury College.

He lives in Orlando, Florida, with his wife Kay, six-year-old daughter, Nikki, two-year-old son, Jonathon, five-year-old dog, Samantha, and too-old-to-count cat, Willie.

DATE DUE

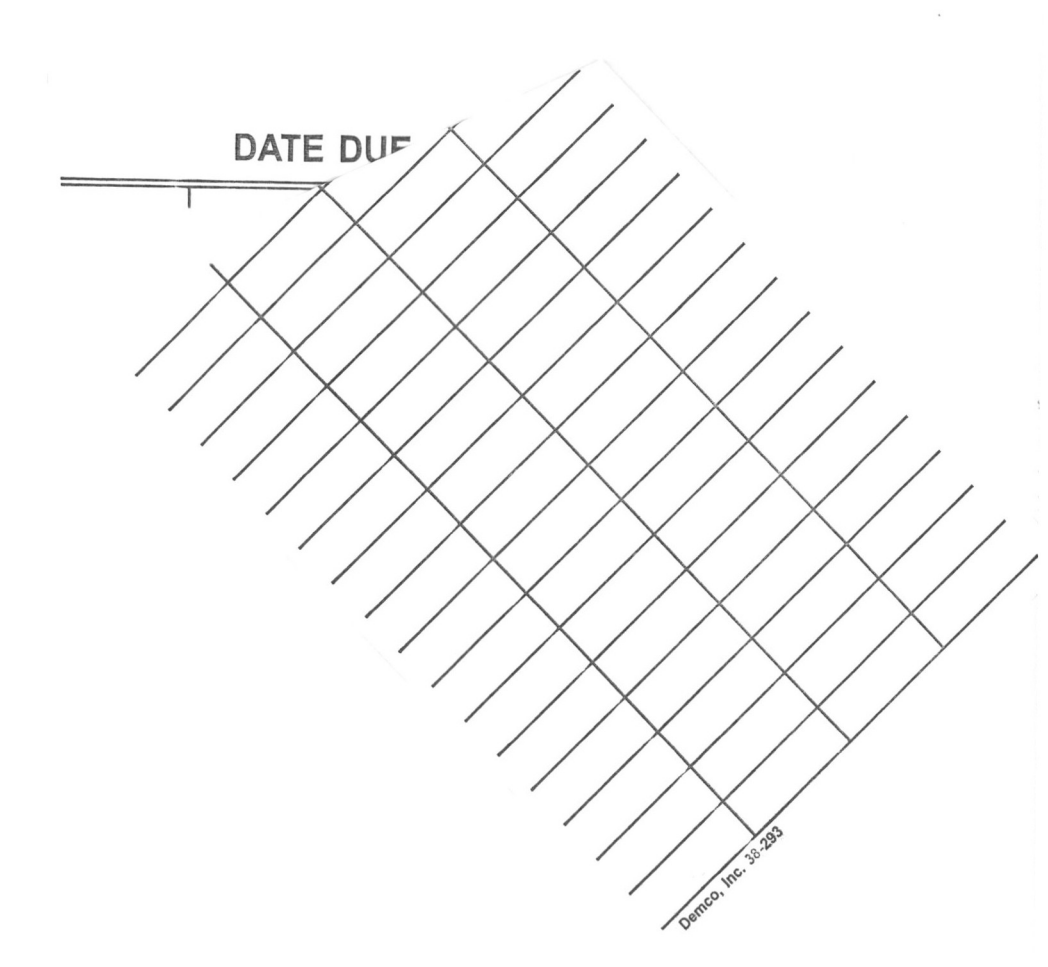